Rodrigo Mazer Etto
Valeska G. Carlos

Social marginalisation in ‘A Polaquinha’ and ‘Stella Manhattan’

Rodrigo Mazer Etto
Valeska G. Carlos

Social marginalisation in 'A Polaquinha' and 'Stella Manhattan'

ScienciaScripts

Imprint
Any brand names and product names mentioned in this book are subject to trademark, brand or patent protection and are trademarks or registered trademarks of their respective holders. The use of brand names, product names, common names, trade names, product descriptions etc. even without a particular marking in this work is in no way to be construed to mean that such names may be regarded as unrestricted in respect of trademark and brand protection legislation and could thus be used by anyone.

Cover image: Provided by the author

This book is a translation from the original published under ISBN 978-3-330-20322-8.

Publisher:
Sciencia Scripts
is a trademark of
Dodo Books Indian Ocean Ltd. and OmniScriptum S.R.L publishing group

120 High Road, East Finchley, London, N2 9ED, United Kingdom
Str. Armeneasca 28/1, office 1, Chisinau MD-2012, Republic of Moldova, Europe
Printed at: see last page
ISBN: 978-620-8-30071-5

Summary

SUMMARY:

From the second half of the 1980s onwards, literature was concerned with portraying the social problems that Brazil was facing with the end of the military regime. In this sense, this work proposes a reflection on the relationship between social marginality and sexuality, using the characters in the book Stella Manhattan (SANTIAGO, 1985) and A polaquinha (TREVISAN, 1985), both published in 1985, the year that marked the end of the military regime in Brazil. Through the methodology of a bibliographical review, and using theoretical references from Lauretis (1994), Beauvoir (2009), Spivak (2010) and Sartre (1993), this work aims to shed light on the question of the social location of subjects, as a result of their sexual orientation. Some theorists, such as Hall (1999, 2000, 2003) and Woodward (2000), who deal with the issue of social identities in post-modernity, will also be presented. Since the aim of this book is to draw a parallel between the two works, the relationship between sexuality and power, according to Foucault (1988, 2007), and the question of patriarchy and the female sex, according to Engels' theoretical assumptions (1980[1934]), will also be pointed out.

Keywords: Homosexuality, female gender, representation.

INTRODUCTION

The idea of working with the works *Stella Manhattan* (SANTIAGO, 1985) and *A polaquinha* (TREVISAN, 1985) was based on the fact that both books were published in 1985, at the end of the military dictatorship[1] , and featured protagonists who were social outcasts because of their sexual orientation and behavior.

Because they represent the spaces and places of the excluded, the peripheral, and allow for the contestation of the socio-cultural and political-economic values that relegate people to social marginality, literature represents a way of denouncing the process of social exclusion that affects those who do not have access to social goods, represented in this book by the characters in the two aforementioned works.

This power to overcome barriers and challenge arbitrary impositions stems from the power of imagination that characterizes literature, because fiction overcomes obstacles and enables people to reflect on their positions and free themselves from repressive behaviour that socially marginalizes those who don't hold the same opinions.

Literature allows different discourses to be represented and individuals to be re-signified within a given cultural context. These individuals can belong to the most prestigious social strata, those who are considered

---

[1] The military dictatorship in Brazil, or the Fifth Brazilian Republic, was the regime established on April 1, 1964 and which lasted until March 15, 1985, under the command of successive military governments. Authoritarian and nationalist in character, it began with the military coup that overthrew the government of Joao Goulart, the then democratically elected president. The regime ended when Josë Sarney took over the presidency, which ushered in the period known as the New Republic (or Sixth Republic). Despite initial promises of a short intervention, the military dictatorship lasted 21 years. Before that, the regime put several Institutional Acts into practice, culminating in Institutional Act Number Five (AI-5) of 1968, which was in force for ten years. The 1946 Constitution was replaced by the 1967 Constitution and, at the same time, the National Congress was dissolved, civil liberties were suppressed and a military criminal procedure code was created that allowed the Brazilian Army and Military Police to arrest and imprison people considered suspicious, in order to make any judicial review impossible.

hegemonic, socially and economically, or they can represent social minorities, those without a voice or a place, those who suffer discrimination and prejudice as a result of the social marginalization in which they find themselves, because they don't fit in with what society considers to be normal or acceptable. These minorities are fighting for recognition of their cultural values.

The analysis of the two works is justified by the need to deconstruct discourses that relegate prostitutes and homosexuals to the margins, excluding them from greater political and social participation.

This work is divided into three parts: the first presents the notes of theorists such as Hall (1999, 2000, 2003) on the process of transformation that the concept of social identity has undergone over recent times.

As this book aims to draw a parallel between the situation of social marginalization - due to sexual orientation and behaviour - between Trevisan's work and Santiago's, the second part provides an overview of the relationship between sexuality and power, using the theoretical contributions of Foucault (1988, 2007).

Considering that social prejudice, which affects marginalized individuals, has as one of its main stimuli the values and traditions of a society based on patriarchal foundations, the third section shows how the theme of patriarchy is approached according to Engels (1980[1934]).

The fourth part discusses how the prostitute woman, represented by the protagonist *Polaquinha*, was portrayed by Trevisan as a male author.

The sixth section looks at the relationship between homosexuality and social marginalization in Stella Manhattan, through the behavior and orientation of its characters.

I. About Silviano Santiago

Born on September 29, 1936 in Formiga, Minas Gerais, writer and literary critic Silviano Santiago is considered one of the most brilliant Brazilian essayists, university professor and literature theorist. At the age of 14, he attended the Centro de Estudos Cinematograficos (CEC) and read Andre Gide's *Os moedeiros falsos* and Fernando Pessoa's *Paginas de doutrina estetica*, books lent to him by his friend and first mentor, Jacques do Prado Brandao.

In 1956, Silviano started a degree course in Neo-Latin Literature at the Federal University of Minas Gerais and wrote poems published under the pseudonym Antonio Nogueira, according to the author, the two names despised by Fernando Pessoa. During his undergraduate studies, he graduated from the French Alliance and became a tutor in French Literature. He received a CAPES grant to specialize in French Literature at the Centre d'Etudes Superieures de Frangais, in Rio de Janeiro, between 1960 and 1961. The specialization in French Literature led Silviano to a doctorate at the University of Paris - Sorbonne, in 1961.

In 1987, he won a post-doctoral scholarship from the CAPES/DAAD program at the University of Cologne, Germany. In 2010, he was awarded the 2010 Minas Gerais Government Prize for Literature for his work as a whole.

Published works

1955-Os velhos (first short story - published in Revista Complemento).

1960- 4 poets (book of poems, published with other authors).

1961- Duas faces (book of short stories published with Ivan Angelo). 1969- Brazil: prose and poetry (Anthology published in New York).

1970 - Salto (poems); O banquete (short stories).

1974- The gaze (novel).

1975- Ariano Suassuna (commented anthology); Iracema (commented edition of Jose de Alencar's novel).

1976 - Carlos Drummond de Andrade (essays); Glossario de Derrida (supervisor of this publication by his master's degree students at PUC-RJ).

1978- Growing up during the war in an overseas province (poems); A literature in the tropics; essays on cultural dependence (essays).

1981- In freedom (novel).

1982- Worth what it weighs; essays on political and cultural issues (essays).

1985 - Stella Manhattan (novel); Poems (Translation of Jacques Prevert's book).

1988- BrasilianischeLiteratur der Zeit der Militarherrschaft (1964-1988), organizer of this work on Brazilian literature from 1964 to 1988.

1989- In the meshes of the letter (essays).

1993- A family story (novel); Journey to Mexico (novel).

1995 - Cheiro forte (poems); Why I love Barthes (Translation of the book by Alain Robbe-Grillet).

1996- Keith Jarrett at the Blue Note (jazz improvisations) (short stories).

1999- De cocoras (novel).

2000- Interpreters of Brazil (organizer of this three-volume work, which brings together texts by authors who have thought about Brazil).

2001- The Space in-between - essaysonLatin American culture (Anthology of essays edited by Ana Lucia Gazzola, at Duke University Press).

2002- Carlos e Mario (organization and notes of the complete correspondence between Mario de Andrade and Carlos Drummond de Andrade).

2003- Republica das Letras, from Gongalves Dias to Ana Cristina Cesar: letters from Brazilian writers: 1965-1995 (organizer).

2004- The Cosmopolitanism of the Poor: Literary Criticism and Cultural Criticism (essays); The False Liar: Memoirs (novel).

2005- Historias Mal Contadas (short stories).

2006- The Roots and Labyrinth of Latin America (essays); Life as Literature: the amanuensis Belmiro (essays).

2008- Herangas (novel).

2010- Anonimos (short stories).

About Dalton Trevisan

Dalton Trevisan is a Brazilian writer. He was awarded the Camoes Prize in 2012 for his work as a whole. He is considered the greatest contemporary Brazilian short story writer. The publication of his book "The Vampire of Curitiba" (1965) earned him the nickname because of his reclusive temperament.

Dalton Jerson Trevisan was born in Curitiba, Parana, on June 14, 1925. He graduated in Law from the Parana Law School. He practiced law for seven years, but gave it up to work in his family's ceramics factory. He made his literary debut with the novel "Sonata ao Luar" (1945). In 1946, he led the literary group in Curitiba that published the literary magazine *Joaquim*, becoming a spokesperson for several writers. He published his second book "Sete Anos de Pastor" in the magazine in 1946.

For several years he produced texts without publishing them. In 1950 he spent six months in Europe. From 1954 onwards, he published his short stories in pamphlet form, in the style of cordel literature, in which he recorded everyday life, especially in the metropole of Curitiba. He published "Guia Historico de Curitiba" and "Cronicas da Provincia de Curitiba".

Trevisan gained national repercussion in 1959 with the publication of

"Novelas Nada Exemplares" (1959), which brought together almost two decades of literary production. He was awarded the Jabuti Prize by the Brazilian Book Chamber. He then published "Cemiterio dos Elefantes" (1964), "O Vampiro de Curitiba" (1965), "A Morte na Praga" (1965) and "Desastres do Amor" (1968). That same year, he won Brazil's biggest literary prize at the 1st National Short Story Competition, sponsored by the State of Paraná.

Dedicated exclusively to short stories, he only had one novel published, "A Polaquinha" (1985). In 1996 he was awarded the Ministerio da Cultura Prize for Literature for his entire body of work. In 2003, he shared the 1st Portugal Telecom Prize for Brazilian Literature with Bernardo de Carvalho, for his book "Pico na Veia".

Dalton Trevisan was the winner of the 24ª edition of the Camoes Prize in 2012.

Announced on May 21st. He was unanimously elected by the jury for his work as a whole. The Camoes Prize is one of the highest honors for Portuguese-language authors. It is a partnership between the governments of Brazil and Portugal, and each year it takes place in one of the two countries.

He also published "The Marital War" (1970), "Crimes of Passion" (1978), "Ah, E" (1994), "The Green-Eyed Maniac" (2008), "Violets and Peacocks" (2009), "Desgracida" (2010), "The Dwarf and the Nymphet" (2011), among others.

In 2003, he shared the country's biggest literary prize with Bernardo Carvalho - the 1st Portugal Telecom Prize for Brazilian Literature - with the book "Pico na Veia".

Published Books[2]

- Abyss of Roses
- Ah, E?
- The Knife in the Heart
- The Marital War
- The Polack
- Drunken macaw
- The Avenging Angel's Trumpet
- Capitu Is Me
- Elephant Cemetery
- 111 Ais
- Chorinho Brejeiro
- Erotic tales
- Crimes of Passion
- Disasters of Love
- Dinora - New Mysteries
- 234
- In Search of Lost Curitiba
- Those Damn Women
- People in Conflict (with Antonio de Alcantara Machado)
- Lincha Tarado
- My Dear Assassin
- Death in Prague
- Mysteries of Curitiba
- Nights of Love in Granada

---

2 All books published by Editora Record - Rio de Janeiro, except "Vozes do Retrato - Quinze Historias de Mentiras e Verdades" and "Quem tem medo de vampiro?", published by Editora Atica - Sao Paulo, "77 Ais", printed by the author on newsprint; "O Grande Deflorador" , "99 Curuiras Nanicas" and "111 Ais", L&PM - Porto Alegre.

- Exemplary Novels
- 99 Nanicas Owls
- The Great Deflower
- The Five-Winged Bird
- The King of the Earth
- The Vampire of Curitiba
- Bread and Blood
- Peak in the vein
- First Book of Short Stories
- Who's afraid of vampires?
- 77Ais
- Twenty Short Stories
- Mad Virgin, Mad Kisses
- Voices from the Portrait - Fifteen Stories of Lies and Truths
- Male does not win flower

II. Postmodern social identity

The heterogeneity that characterizes each and every discourse manifests itself both in the extralingulistic dimension - every discourse carries other discourses within it - and in the intralingulistic dimension - discourses are marked by contradictions and imperfections that reflect the fallibility and internal conflicts of the subjects who produced them. For Grigoletto:

> "Talking about heterogeneity means, first of all, questioning the uniqueness of all speech, considering the presence of the other in the constitution of each and every discourse, which means postulating ideology and power relations as constitutive of social relations. To deny these manifestations is to camouflage and mask the presence of heterogeneity. Finally, speaking of heterogeneity also means considering the meanings as multiple and the subject as split, dispersed" (GRIGOLETTO, 2005, p. 125).

The question of the decentering of the subject has been addressed by a number of authors from various disciplines over the last few decades. The first part of Stuart Hall's *Cultural Identity in Postmodernity* is one of the places where the subject is dealt with most clearly and didactically, which is why this text serves as a theoretical contribution to the discussion of the crisis of *postmodern* identities.

The key expression in Hall's text is *identity crisis.* The period of late modernity, or post-modernity, is marked by the shaking of old, stable cultural identities on which individuals rely in their social interactions. What is to be understood by the term *identity crisis;* what events precipitated this crisis; what are its forms and what are its potential consequences - these are some of the questions that Hall asks and tries to answer.

Hall starts from the assumption that the modern subject is undergoing a process of *decentering*, which consists of the displacement or fragmentation of modern identities. He refers more specifically to what he calls *cultural identities* - *"those aspects of our identities that arise from our 'belonging' to ethnic, racial, linguistic, religious and, above all, national cultures"* (HALL, 1999, p. 8).

After warning that his book is an open work and subject to challenge - an attitude, like Bakhtin's (1986, 2002, 2003, 2007, 2008), which accepts dialogue, and admitting that the concept of identity itself is still underdeveloped in the social sciences, Hall formulates the central argument of his book in the following terms:

> A different kind of structural change is transforming modern societies at the end of the 20th century. This is fragmenting the cultural landscapes of class, gender, sexuality, ethnicity, race and nationality, which in the past had provided us with solid locations as social individuals. These transformations are also changing our personal identities, shaking the idea we have of ourselves as integrated subjects. This loss of a stable 'sense of self' is sometimes called the displacement or decentering of the subject. This double displacement - the disembedding of individuals both from their place in the social and cultural world and from themselves - constitutes an 'identity crisis' for the individual (HALL, 1999, p. 9).

To support his argument, Hall distinguishes three types of subject, each with its own particular conception of identity: the Enlightenment subject, the sociological subject and the post-modern subject.

The Enlightenment subject (usually described as male) was based on an individualistic conception of identity, the "center" of which was born with the individual and remained unchanged throughout their existence.

The sociological subject was based on a more interactive conception of identity: the inner core of the subject was not an autonomous and self-sufficient entity, but was affirmed through their social relationships, in other words, their insertion into a certain culture. Identity would be precisely the line that "sutures" the subject to the structure in which they live.

The postmodern subject is the result of a process of multiple fragmentations. Not only are the old unified and stable identities fragmenting, but also the very cultural structures to which these identities were related are collapsing. The very process of identification between subject and cultural identity would have become more provisional and more problematic.

As a product of this process, the identity of the post-modern subject becomes a *mobile,* historically defined *celebration*, formed in reaction to the constant changes in the cultural systems in which the subject is inserted. The individual is not formed by one identity, but by several contradictory ones. A unified identity is nothing more than an illusion, supported by a fanciful *narrative of the self:*

> Instead, as systems of meaning and cultural representation multiply, we are confronted by a bewildering and changing multiplicity of possible identities, each of which we could identify with - at least temporarily (HALL, 1999, p. 13).

Hall draws attention to the importance of change in late modernity. Everything is uncertain, temporary; everything changes at a rapid pace; crises follow one another. *"Modern societies are therefore, by definition, societies of constant, rapid and permanent change"* (HALL, 1999, p. 14). For Hall, this is the essential characteristic of modern societies, what distinguishes them from traditional societies.

This change, however, has even more profound consequences when you take into account that it doesn't happen from a single nucleus, from a central, unified organizing principle: unlike traditional societies, modern society is decentralized, discontinuous, fragmented; it has several centers of power that constantly influence and move in relation to each other.

Ernest Laclau (1993, 2001) and cited by Hall as one of the scholars who have argued that the tension caused by the various centers of power is reflected in individuals in the form of different *subject positions,* adopted in different social contexts.

The disintegration of these societies and identities does not occur because they are able to articulate and balance themselves. Although this articulation is always precarious, temporary and partial, its effects can be positive, since new identities and new subjects can emerge that are better adapted to the new social structures.

Hall approaches the problem of the modern subject as a *historical problem* the three conceptions he attributes to the subject throughout modernity are historically determined and make up a narrative of the transformations undergone by the human subject. Hall demonstrates that this discursive figure called the modern subject is an entity that is constantly being transformed.
shaped according to the characteristics of each historical moment.

The period from roughly the Renaissance[3] to the
The Enlightenment[4] is identified by Hall as the birthplace of the modern concept of the subject. The conception that emerges from it is of an

3 Renaissance is a term used to identify the period of European history roughly between the end of the 14th century and the end of the 16th century, marked by transformations in many areas of human life. It was called the "Renaissance" because of the rediscovery and revaluation of the cultural references of classical antiquity, which guided the changes of this period towards a humanist and naturalist ideal. The term was first recorded by Giorgio Vasari *in* the 16th century, but the concept of Renaissance, as we understand it today, emerged with the publication of Jacob Burckhardt's book *The Culture of the Renaissance in Italy* (1867), in which he defined the period as a time of "discovery of the world and of man".

4 The Enlightenment, also known as the Age of Enlightenment, was a cultural movement of the European intellectual elite of the 18th century that sought to mobilize the power of reason in order to reform society and the knowledge inherited from the medieval tradition. It encompassed a number of tendencies and, among them, it sought an accurate knowledge of nature, with the aim of making it useful to modern, progressive man. It promoted intellectual exchange and opposed the intolerance of the Church and the State.

individualized subject, whose identity is no longer determined by his or her stable links to traditions or structures. The subject is no longer conceived as just *another brick in the wall,* a simple peg in a larger institutional system; it is a unique, indivisible, singular entity, distinct from all others.

This notion of the subject, one of the hallmarks of modernity, owes its emergence to certain schools of thought of that period: the Reformation and Protestantism, which removed the institutional intermediary in the relationship between the individual and divinity; Renaissance Humanism, which declared Man (the inclusion of Woman would still take some time...) as the center of the universe; the scientific revolutions, which provided human beings with the tools to systematically explore and unravel the mysteries of nature; and the Enlightenment, which bet on the human being as the center of the universe....) as the center of the universe; the scientific revolutions, which provided human beings with the tools to systematically explore and unravel the mysteries of nature; and the Enlightenment, which bet on the power of rationality and enlightenment to combat ignorance and intellectual dogmas.

Rene Descartes (1 9 9 6) placed the individual subject at the heart of his philosophical system. The individual's ability to reason was the ground zero of knowledge; the watchword of the Cartesian subject was the emphatic motto *"cogito, ergo sum"* - "I think, therefore I am".

John Locke (1999) defined the individual as possessing an identity whose essence would be unalterable; a sovereign individual, the source of reason, action and knowledge at one end, and the subject of the consequences of these practices at the other.

The rise of the individualist subject seems to have originated in the reaction to the social, economic and religious order of medieval feudalist society, as Raymond Williams (1983) argues. The repudiation of the social hierarchy of the feudal system, the strengthening of a new type of commerce, based on the individual and private property, and the emphasis on the direct relationship between the believer and his god defended by Protestantism created the conditions for the widespread dissemination of the Enlightenment conception of the subject.

In the 19th century, the Enlightenment subject gave way to the sociological subject. The growing complexity of modern societies - especially urban ones - the advent of the nation-state, the emergence of large population masses and the industrialization of Europe and the United States led to the articulation of a new conception of the subject. The individual came to be analyzed as part of a social organism that demanded his participation; the citizen *"became entangled in the bureaucratic and administrative machinery of the modern state"* (HALL, 1999, p. 30). Important aspects of the previous conception remained in vogue; rather than the total replacement of one model by the other, what occurred was the adoption of an approach that took more account of the social integration and interaction of individuals.

The notion of a sociological subject was supported by two movements. The first was Darwinian biology, which attributed the foundations of human reason and mind to nature and biology.

The second was the emergence of the new social sciences. Psychology was in charge of studying the individual's mental processes, while the other social sciences, especially sociology, explained the subject in terms of their relationships in society. This *theory of socialization* provided *"an alternative explanation of the way in which individuals are subjectively formed through their participation in wider social relations; and, conversely, of the way in which processes and structures are sustained by the roles that individuals play in them"* (HALL, 1999, p. 31).

Paradoxically, while contesting the Cartesian, rational and individualistic subject as a fiction, social scientists such as G. H. Mead (1970), Goffman (1998) and Parsons (2013) did not escape the dualistic categorization that opposed individual and society, interior and exterior.

The first decades of the 20th century saw the emergence of a new individual - *""isolated, exiled or alienated, set against the background of the anonymous and impersonal crowd or metropole"* (HALL, 1999, p. 32). The artistic and intellectual movements that made up Modernism show the representations that were made of this type of individual: Baudelaire's *painter of modern life* (2006), Franz Kafka's *Josef K.* (1997) and the *flaneur* portrayed by Walter Benjamin (1986) in his essay on Baudelaire's Paris, are some examples of the change that the subject of the Enlightenment and the sociological subject would undergo throughout the 20th century.

It was in late modernity - the second half of the last century - that the post-modern conception of the subject was consolidated. Characterized by a fragmented identity, isolated and alienated in the face of the immensity of the modern metropole, and dislocated from his social place and from himself, the postmodern subject is the result of transformations in the sphere of thought and social action which, in Hall's opinion, are well represented by five major advances in the human sciences and social theory: Marxism, Freudism, Saussure's linguistics, Michel Foucault's thought and feminism.

These five bodies of ideas were mainly responsible for "a series of ruptures in the discourses of modern knowledge" and, consequently, for *"the final decentering of the Cartesian subject"* (HALL, 1999, p. 34).

The first of the conceptual ruptures identified by Hall is the legacy of

Karl Marx. According to his interpreters in the second half of the 20th century, Marx removed the centrality of history from the individual subject and transferred it to social relations; the individual's ability to make history would be determined by the structural conditions in which he acts. Louis Althusser (1980) is one of the Marxist theorists who echoed Marx's displacement of the subject by rejecting the idea that man has a *universal essence* and that this essence is a singular and unique attribute of each individual. Although this anti-humanist position has been widely contested, it has nevertheless had a major influence on modern thought.

The second major blow to the Cartesian subject was dealt by Freud (1905, 1915). By discovering the unconscious, Freud displaced the centrality of the Enlightenment subject in at least two respects: firstly, by arguing that our desires and sexuality - the fundamental components of our identities - do not obey the laws of reason, but a very particular *logic that* is absolutely distinct from Cartesian logic; and secondly, by proposing that the structure of our psyche is far from being unified and fixed - on the contrary, it is made up of several layers that constantly influence and modify each other: "*identity is really something formed over time through unconscious processes, rather than something innate, existing in consciousness at birth*" (HALL, 1999, p. 38). 38). For psychoanalysts, the feeling of a unified self is nothing more than an illusion, a *"fantasy of the self",* created by the individual in order to recover a *"fantasized pleasure of plenitude"* (HALL, 1999, p. 39).

The third rupture examined by Hall was caused by the influence of Ferdinand de Saussure's work on thinkers such as Lacan (1998[1949], [1957]) and Derrida (1978). Saussure's proposition that
meanings are based on difference *(night* is something that is not *day,* and vice versa) is reflected in the conception of the *self* as something that is not the

other. As the meaning of words is not fixed (it arises precisely from these relations of difference, which destabilize it and prevent its definitive closure), neither can identity be definitively fixed - it is constantly disturbed by *""difference""* - the individual's relationship with the other and with the stimuli of the outside world: *""despite his best efforts, the individual speaker can never fix the meaning of a final form, including the meaning of his identity""* (HALL, 1999, p. 41). 41).

Michel Foucault is indicated by Hall as being responsible for the fourth decentering of the rational subject. Foucault's work, developed largely around the concept of *disciplinary power*, undermines the belief in the existence of a rational, intellectually free and self-determined subject. Foucault argues that modern institutions - hospitals, schools, barracks, prisons, hospices - have a strongly police and disciplinary character and thus seek to maintain strict control over the activities of individuals - their work, their thoughts, their pleasures, their sexual practices. Although these institutions use the strategy of *individualizing* the subject as a way of improving control (by assigning them an ID number, for example), this individualization does not turn into a stable identity, but into alienation and submission to a bureaucratic and impersonal system.

The theory and practice of feminism constitute, in Hall's view, the fifth and final blow to the subject of the Enlightenment. Hall places feminism among the social movements that grew stronger throughout the 1960s and were characterized by *identity politics,* in which each movement relied on the social identity of its members - *"feminism appealed to women, sexual politics to gays and lesbians, racial struggles to blacks, the anti-bellum movement to pacifists, and so on"* (HALL, 1999, p. 45).

It is clear that the Enlightenment subject - in essence, a white, heterosexual male subject - was profoundly shaken by the demands of these movements, in particular the feminist movement. Feminism argued that the separation between public and private was an illusion, advocated the politicization of spheres that had historically been infested with politics (sexuality, domestic life, childcare), argued that the definition of identities (including sexual identities) was a political process and questioned the idea of a unified humanity in which all questions of sexual difference would be appeased.

III. Sexuality and power

Stuart Hall believes in the close relationship between socio-economic phenomena and symbolic manifestations. Although he rejects the simplistic view defended by some more radical theorists, who, based on a classic metaphor of revolutionary transformation, argued that *""when social hierarchies are overthrown, an inversion of cultural values and symbols has to take place sooner or later"* (HALL, 2003, p. 220), the author is sympathetic to alternative metaphors, such as the Bakhtinian concepts of carvanalization and dialogism. For Hall, *Marxism and the Philosophy of Language ""played a critical role in the general theoretical shift from what might have remained a flirtation with a version, however modified, of the 'base and superstructure' metaphor, to a conception of the ideological fully focused on discourse-and-poded*" (HALL, 2003, p. 232).

This conception of ideology based on the relationship between power and knowledge is one of the strong points of the work of French thinker Michel Foucault.

In the first volume of his *History of Sexuality,* entitled *The Will to Know,* Foucault deals with the discourse on sex and sexual repression that emerged in the 17th century during the rise of the bourgeoisie and capitalism.

Foucault defends the existence of an "economy", a series of "interests" that support the thesis that the relationship between power and sex is one of repression. For Foucault, sexuality is a *dispositive,* which he defines as a

> a decidedly heterogeneous whole that encompasses discourses, institutions, architectural organizations, decisions regulations, laws, administrative measures, scientific statements, philosophical, moral and philanthropic propositions. In short, the said and the unsaid are the elements of the device. The device is the network that can be established between these elements (FOUCAULT, 2007, p. 244).

In *The Will to Know,* Foucault challenges what he calls the *"repressive hypothesis"* - if sex is so repressed, why do we talk about it so much, and in such detail? And "*why do we blame ourselves so much for having once made it a sin?"* (FOUCAULT, 1988, p. 14). His intention is not to show, in advance, that the repressive hypothesis is false, but "to *place it in a global economy of discourses on sex within modern societies from the 18th century onwards.* He doesn't want to show *what,* but *how*: by which paths power reaches desire in individuals, "how *power penetrates and controls everyday pleasure"* (FOUCAULT, 1988, p. 16).

Foucault does not deny that prohibition and repression exist. What he actually disputes is that considering interdiction as a fundamental element in the elaboration of the history of sexuality is an illusion. The negative elements of the repressive hypothesis (prohibitions, censures, denials) "are only handles that have a local and tactical function in a discursive placement, in a technique of power, in a will to know that is far from being reduced to this" (FOUCAULT, 1988, p. 17).

In the 17th, 18th and 19th centuries, what Foucault identifies as a "discursive explosion" of sexual issues took place. Although situations of silence, tact and discourse arose (for example, between parents and children, or between educators and students), discourses on sex, both licit and illicit, did not stop proliferating.

Christianity seeks to transform sex into discourse through confession. The descriptive detail initially prescribed by the Christian religion unfolds and continues until Sade and the erotic authors of the late 19th century. Although the discourses have different intentions, for Foucault they belong to the same tradition:

> The essential thing is this: that Western man for three centuries

> has remained tied to this task of saying everything about his sex; that, from the classical era onwards, there has been a constant increase and an ever greater valorization of the discourse on sex; and that this discourse, carefully analyzed, has been expected to have multiple effects of displacement, intensification, of reorientation, modification of desire itself. Not only was the domain of what could be said about sex widened and men forced to extend it more and more, but, above all, discourse was focused on sex, through a complete device with varied effects that cannot be exhausted in a simple relationship with a law of interdiction. Censorship of sex? On the contrary, an apparatus has been set up to produce discourses on sex, more and more discourses, capable of functioning and of being the effect of their own economy (FOUCAULT, 1988, p. 26).

In the 18th century, a *rational* discourse on sex was formulated. This analytical discourse soon took on *police* form, meaning that sex was regulated through *useful* and *Ptolemaic* discourses, rather than through a strict policy of prohibition. Foucault offers some examples of this process. The emergence of the concept of "population" led to the emergence of the economic analysis of sexual behavior, which measures birth rates, frequency of sexual relations, among others. In another example, Foucault cites the schools of the 18th century. Although sex is not *talked about*, it is present in the *silences* - in the architecture, in the regulations, in the constant surveillance of the institution. Erotic literature and court cases against "perverts" show that

> from one extreme to another, sex has become, in any case, something that must be said, and said exhaustively, according to different discursive devices, but all constraining, each in its own way. Subtle confidence or authoritarian interrogation, sex, refined or rustic, must be said (FOUCAULT, 1988, p. 34).

What should be noted is that this growth of erotic discourse took place *within* power, not outside it or against it. It was power itself that stimulated the proliferation of discourses on sex; *"everywhere, incitements to speak were created; everywhere, devices for listening and recording, procedures for observing, questioning and formulating. They [sex] were de-furnished and forced into a discursive existence"* (FOUCAULT, 1988, p. 34).

Foucault stresses that there is not just one, but several discourses on sex. In the Middle Ages, the discourse was unified: concupiscence led to first-person confession. In modern times, this single discourse has given way to multiple discourses - biology, demography, medicine and psychiatry. There is no longer any concern about hiding sex in a church confessional. Instead, there are stimuli to deal with it in all the relevant discourses, in a regulated and multiform way.

Behind this discursive phenomenon of the last three centuries, Foucault identifies not the evidence of a "fundamental interdiction", but an interest in giving sex a certain secret, hidden aura. The characteristic of modern societies *"is not that they have condemned sex to remain in obscurity, but that they have devoted themselves to always talking about it, valuing it as the secret"* (FOUCAULT, 1988, p. 36).

The multiplication of discourses on sex, Foucault speculates, would have the objective of *"providing an economically viable and politically conservative sexuality"* (FOUCAULT, 1988, p. 38), removing from reality sexual manifestations not aimed at reproduction.

Until the end of the 18th century, three codes (in addition to customs) governed sexual practices: canon law, Christian pastoral care and civil law. Thus, *"prohibitions relating to sex were fundamentally of a juridical nature"* (FOUCAULT, 1988, p. 39). The proliferation of discourses on sex is marked, in the 18th and 19th centuries, by the voice given to the discourse *of peripheral sexualities*, i.e. everything outside heterosexual monogamy. *Regular sexuality* is now seen only in contrast to peripheral sexualities. What was once simply debauchery now goes by various names: *genital neurosis, aberration of the genetic sense, degeneracy, psychic imbalance.*

Foucault identifies two historical procedures for producing the truth of sex. On the one hand, the *ars erotica* is the proper procedure of ancient civilizations and values mystery, secrecy and initiation. On the other hand, the *scientia sexualis* is typical of modern Western civilization and has confession as its privileged technique for producing truth. Foucault sees serious dangers in the approach favored by the West. In the first place, confession is an institution that, at various times in history, has gone hand in hand with torture, a duo that Foucault calls "sinister twins". By becoming, according to Foucault, a "confiding animal", man has seen confession become an instrument not of liberation, but of subjection.

Confession has changed over time. From penance, it has become other things, less ritual and exclusive: "The motivations and effects expected of it have diversified, as have the forms it takes: interrogations, consultations, autobiographical narratives or letters, which are recorded, transcribed, collected in files, published and commented on" (FOUCAULT, 1988, p. 62).

By breaking with the procedures of the *ars erotica*, "our society has constituted a *scientia sexualis.* More precisely, it has given itself the task of producing true discourses on sex, and this by trying to adjust, not without difficulty, the ancient procedure of confession to the rules of scientific discourse" (FOUCAULT, 1988, p. 66).

The production of these "true discourses on sex" involves, for Foucault, the formation of a kind of knowledge whose foundation is not in repression or the law, but in *power.* The concepts of truth and power are mutually determining, insofar as truth, according to Foucault, can be defined as *"the power proper to discourses accepted as true"* (FOUCAULT, 2007, p. 231).

One of the central themes in Foucault's work, power received a very personal definition from the French philosopher. It is a concept of great capillarity and social penetration, which exerts its influence at various levels and in various directions. "Power is everywhere; not because it encompasses everything, but because it comes from everywhere". Power is a correlation of "unbalanced, heterogeneous, unstable, tense" forces; it is not an institution, nor a structure, nor a type of gift; power is "the name given to a complex strategic situation in a given society" (FOUCAULT, 1988, p. 89).

Foucault sees power as a large network, without a center, complex, mobile, in which resistance plays a fundamental role - in fact, resistances are also mobile and transient. *"It is in this field of correlations of force that one must try to analyze the mechanisms of power"* (FOUCAULT, 1988, p. 92). The question to ask is: what power relations are at play in discourses on sex? To answer it, we need to *"immerse the exuberant production of discourses on sex in the field of power relations, which are multiple and mobile"* (FOUCAULT, 1988, p. 93).

IV. Patriarchy and the question of feminism

Foucault argued that the multiplicity of discourses on sex did not only obey a purely enlightening and scientific intention (knowledge), but also political purposes (power). Like Stuart Hall (2003), Foucault (2007) establishes a close relationship between knowledge and power - between the symbolic manifestations of culture and the social forces that determine the behavior of individuals: "*power transforms the fundamental archaeological structures (epistemes or discursive formations) that underlie our knowledge*" (GUTTING, 2005, p. 50).

The imbalance of power that forms the core of patriarchal society has, of course, been reproduced in all manifestations of Western culture, including literature. The literary canon of the West can be read as a history of patriarchy - of its supremacy over a good part of the last twenty-odd centuries; of the sporadic and isolated attempts to weaken and overthrow it; and, finally, of what appears to be its decline - a process that has gained momentum over the last century and shows no signs of weakening.

Scholars who have dedicated themselves to the subject of patriarchy and its origins have inevitably come up against the following question: what existed before patriarchal society? The available archaeological evidence is insufficient to decisively confirm the hypothesis that, before patriarchy, human beings were organized in matriarchal societies.

The abundance of images of female deities produced by ancient peoples, for example, says little, strictly speaking, about the way these societies organized and governed themselves. The valorization of women as symbols of fertility, especially at a time when the role of men in reproduction had not yet been discovered, is not sufficient evidence that human beings have generally organized themselves into social systems in which women held the main positions of leadership and power. There are indications that societies in specific places and times have experimented with matriarchal models of organization, as is the case in ancient times with the Minoan civilization and, today, with peoples in China and Indonesia. These cases, however, can be seen as exceptions that confirm the rule: patriarchy, as far as history records, is the predominant form of social organization in human groupings.

Friedrich Engels (1980[1934]) argued that at some remote point in the past, human beings organized themselves into societies in which women were equal to men in terms of power and leadership. Engels applied the thesis of historical materialism to the study of the origins of patriarchy and the result was published under the title *The Origin of Family, Private Property and the State.*

With all the criticism and challenges it has received in the almost 130 years since it was first published (some from intellectuals of the caliber of Simone de Beauvoir), Engels' book remains one of the main references for studies on patriarchy, from a political and socio-economic perspective.

The man, owner of the most valuable goods, demanded fidelity from the woman as a way of ensuring paternity of the children to whom his inheritance was destined. The guarantee of this fidelity meant, strictly speaking, the inclusion of the woman among the list of man's possessions; he now had the power of life and death over her - a right he would preserve for centuries to come. In Engels' words, patriarchy

> [...] it is based on the predominance of the man; its express purpose is to procreate children whose paternity is indisputable; and this indisputable paternity is required because the children, as direct heirs, will one day come into possession of their father's property....) The man is also granted the right to marital infidelity,

> sanctioned at least by custom (the Code of Napoleon expressly grants it, as long as he doesn't bring the concubine to the marital home), and this right is exercised more and more widely as society evolves. When a woman happens to remember old sexual practices and tries to renew them, she is punished more rigorously than in any previous era (ENGELS, 1980, p. 66).

The close relationship that Engels established between the economic, political and moral aspects of the domination of men over women made him one of the strongest defenders of the idea that patriarchy is a historically determined phenomenon, and not a natural fact that has accompanied human society since its origins, as can be seen in the following statement

> The collapse of maternal rights, the great historical defeat of the female sex throughout the world. The man also took over the running of the household; the woman was degraded, turned into a servant, a slave to the man's lust, a simple instrument of reproduction. This low condition of woman, manifested above all among the Greeks of heroic times and even more so among those of classical times, has gradually been retouched, concealed and, in certain places, even clothed in forms of greater softness, but by no means suppressed (ENGELS, 1980 [1934], p. 61).

The different discourses on patriarchy presented in this chapter offer a sample overview of the treatments this theme has received in the human sciences. They will serve as support for the analysis in the next chapter - the study of the marginalized situation of women through Dalton Trevisan's prostitute character.

V. Dalton Trevisan's polaquinha

Literature allows hegemonically positioned paradigms to be challenged, destabilizing ideas and values, laying bare aspects of social life that have remained hidden and demand a more critical look from society.

In the history of societies, both ancient and contemporary, there are many examples of censorship serving as an instrument of repression and policing, preventing free cultural expression and silencing narratives that addressed important issues related to marginalized social groups. For this reason, literature can represent a threat to the social order, because it is through literature that it is possible to question traditionalism and the imposition of certain values, which marginalize those who have no voice or place.

In this sense, the book *A polaquinha* deals with a theme strictly related to social marginality, presenting the issue of prostitutes in the context of Curitiba society. In this work, the writer Dalton Trevisan deals with pornography in a naturalized way, symbolized in the role of the character who gives the book its name.

Other writers have tackled themes linked to social marginalization: Joao Antonio (1986, 2004), through an affective treatment and a strong relationship of identity with the world he portrays, presented the vision of the rascal; Rubem Fonseca (1975, 1979), by creating a narrative from the point of view of characters in debt to the law, exposes dramas arising from the transgressive attitudes and behavior of his characters, and his book *Happy New Year* was banned from circulation throughout the country and collected by the Federal Police Department, on the grounds that it contained content contrary to morals and good customs. These are all writers with a literary background who have adopted the voice of otherness in their works.

If Rubem Fonseca fits into a first level of literature related to peripheral characters, and Joao Antonio is located in a second literary level of this type of approach, Dalton represents a third level, because in the work in question the social marginalization to which his characters are relegated is represented by the vision of the prostitute.

Some authors have already raised important aspects of Trevisan's book, such as Professor Miguel Sanches Neto (1994) in his master's dissertation entitled *O Artificio Obsceno: visita a polaquinha* (NETO, 1994), which deals with a prostitute from Curitiba who, as she discovers the mysteries of sexuality, offers her narrative to the reader.

The very title of the book already demonstrates that it is the story of a woman, the prostitute protagonist, who, by starring in and narrating her story, represents the feminine, seen and constructed from a male perspective, that of the author.

The protagonist introduces her clients, starting with Joao, her first lover who gave her the first theoretical teachings on sex; then it's Tito's turn to have a relationship with the Polish woman; her third partner is Nando, and she finishes her exchange of partners with Pedro.

The story is told by the character herself, who in addition to sexual power, has the power of speech in the narrative. Reading the book gives the sensation that the Polish woman is telling her story to the reader, who can be considered another client who, by hiring her sexual services through reading, develops a close and intimate relationship with the Polish woman, as can be seen in the passage "His portrait his mother tore up, otherwise I'd show it to you" (TREVISAN, 1985, p.25).

At times, this closeness between her and the reader takes on traces of confidences, of secrets being revealed, as in the passages: "If my mother goes up the stairs, you'll see?" (TREVISAN, 1985, p. 11), "What a fool, I'll come back for you?" (TREVISAN, 1985, p.15). This closeness and trust that is established between the reader and the protagonist suggests a false intimacy, very close to the relationship that is established between a client and a prostitute, where intimacy is restricted to the sexual act itself, and does not constitute a manifestation of affective intimacy.

When he tells us about his first boyfriend, Joao, we can see that Dalton Trevisan represents the character through the appropriation of his languages: "He hugged me, I trembled with pleasure. So much fear: hard, big, piercing my pants" (TREVISAN, 1985, p. 10), "I wanted to, but he would only touch me" (TREVISAN, 1985, p.11), and he incorporates, in a serious literature, characters who are not taken seriously, presenting the subalterns through seductive language.

In the representation of the prostitute woman, Trevisan constructs the figure of the protagonist through the lens of her own masculine gender identity, reproducing a discourse that preaches the superiority of men over women, especially in matters relating to sexuality, as can be seen in the passage in which the Polish girl insists that Joao explain some matters relating to sex: "What do you want to know so much? When you get married, you'll learn" (TREVISAN, 1985, p.14). This passage reinforces the idea of male supremacy and hegemony by indicating that men, unlike women, naturally learn the mysteries of sexuality.

According to Teresa de Lauretis (1994), the category of gender was developed by contemporary feminist theorists with the aim of understanding and responding to the situation of inequality between the sexes and how this situation interferes with social relations as a whole. From this perspective, the conceptions of male and female, in which all human beings are classified, form a gender system in each culture, which relates sex to cultural content according to social values and hierarchies:

> The construction of gender is as much a product as the process of its representation." For her, the "sex-gender system, in short, is as much a socio-cultural construction as it is a semiotic apparatus, a system of representations that attributes meaning (identity, value, prestige, kinship position, status within the social hierarchy, etc.) to individuals within society. If gender representations are social positions that carry differential meanings, then the fact that someone is represented or represents themselves as male or female implies the totality of those social attributes (LAURETIS, 1994, p. 212).

Dalton Trevisan demonstrates that the fact that the character felt a lot of affection for her first boyfriend was because he explained some sexual issues to her: "My passion was the same. Not passion, which is fleeting. Love" (TREVISAN, 1985, p. 13), represents the man teaching the woman, which can be interpreted, in parallel, as a male element prescribing or suggesting the behavior of a woman, in this case the prostitute.

After she manages to get back together with Joao, who resists her suggestion that they go to a hotel and then gives in, he treats her in an extremely rude and indelicate manner: "- You're not pure anymore. You're not a virgin anymore. You never were." (TREVISAN, 1985, p.19). This passage reproduces a very common male behavior, culturally ingrained in society with sexist values, where immediately after the sexual act, the man takes on a colder, harsher tone, unlike the female behavior, which usually shows affection and affection towards her partner after a sexual relationship, and even taking into account the protagonist's role as a prostitute, it is possible to see the symbolic construction of the concept of the objectification of women.

Paradoxically, the protagonist's desire to be sexually initiated with Joao, her first love, reflects a certain contestation with a discourse that preaches that prostitute women have no feelings and therefore don't connect with anyone affectively.

Another interesting point to note is that the importance of female virginity for men coincides with the construction of a value that separates women into those who are suitable for more serious relationships, in this case virgins, and those who are not suitable for marriage, because they have already had sexual experiences.

Joao's harsh and offensive speech after the sexual act demonstrates his position according to the definition of the right woman and the wrong woman, and when he calls her impure he reproduces a discourse that has historically placed her in a position of subalternity, because the representation of women has always been made from a male perspective, which contributed to the female element being excluded from all socio-political and cultural participation until the 19th century.

But it's worth remembering that it's through Dalton that the polka-dot girl speaks, and although the reader can imagine the character's humiliation at hearing Joao's words, it's not a woman who is behind the representation of the character, it's Dalton, a man.

On the occasion when Polaquinha resents the fact that Joao has reached orgasm and she hasn't: "With raw anger, because he succeeded, I didn't. Selfish, if he told me, who knows? Selfish, if he'd let me know, who knows?" (TREVISAN, 1985, p. 16), as well as showing that the sexist discourse prioritizes male pleasure over female sexual ecstasy, this passage can be interpreted as a reproduction of the idea of social gender inequality, which relates the image of women to the sexual obligation to give pleasure to men.

In this sense, according to Mireya Suarez (2000, p. 26-27), as well as making it possible to deconstruct the relationship between women and biological nature, the concept of gender makes it possible to distinguish and describe social categories and explain the relationships established between them.

Despite being a sex worker, it can be inferred that Dalton reproduced this discourse of traditionalist and patriarchal values, because as a man, it would be impossible for him to perfectly reproduce the traits, behaviors and feelings that motivate women's actions and, although he addresses other female characters in his works, he doesn't speak exactly from this peripheral place that women, both prostitutes and others, are socioculturally located.

Another important point is that bringing a woman to orgasm is a condition disregarded by most men, who consider them to be a kind of commodity for satisfying male sexual urges and, even as a sex worker, the little octopus had feelings for John, for her their relationship was affective, and yet John was only concerned with giving vent to his own sexual urges.

After a frustrating relationship with her first boyfriend, Joao, the protagonist is disappointed again when she gets involved with a married man named Tito. When she meets another married man called Nando, a lawyer, she has her first orgasm and ends up falling in love with him:

> "I couldn't see myself without Nando. He was more than anything - the brother I didn't have, the father who didn't die. I couldn't buy an earring without talking to him. He taught me how to dress. He made me change my hair. [...] One day he'd come close, the next he'd kiss me. Sometimes just a little, sometimes not at all. Until one night, really crazy, I let him (TREVISAN, 1985, p. 40).

In the passage above, it is also possible to see the subordinate position of the protagonist created by Trevisan, since it is possible to see the relationship of dependence created between the polka-dot girl and Nando, who resents the lack of a male presence, whether in the social role of husband, father or brother.

Within the context of subalternity, Gayatri C. Spivak (2010, p.84) states that female subalternity "seems to be the most problematic", it has been constituted

as a double dumbness, because it arises through a double imposition of imperialist and patriarchal ideologies.

The main character's subordinate position is evident not only because of her feminine nature, but also because of her social position as a prostitute, which causes male desires and fantasies to break down her weak intimate barriers, as can be seen in the passage in which Nando insists on anal sex:

> Be nice. Leave it, darling. Just the tip. If it hurts, I'll take it off. Didn't you do it? Horrible, it hurt like hell. I cried. I remembered my mother. Never let her do that. It ruins the woman. She ends up dying. Dried out and broken (TREVISAN, 1985, p. 56).

Reading the book pulls the reader into the narrative, and its narrative structure features one speech starting in the middle of another, further reinforcing the effect of speech used in a real situation. By incorporating orality, in which compound sentences are reduced to simple sentences, with the abuse of periods, and by using distinctly regional terms, Dalton creates literature with a language very close to that used in everyday speech, bringing his work closer to the concept of the "zero degree of writing" (BARTHES, 1984), in which it would be considered literature only from this level of language, and not what was below it.

The use of language closer to real speech, through the voices of socially marginalized characters, was also a resource adopted in Stella Manhattan (SANTIAGO, 1985), and although its narrative deals with the issue of sexuality, its theme is directed towards the homosexuality of its characters during the repressive period of the military dictatorship. Both books were published in 1985, a period that marked the end of the military regime in Brazil.

VI. Stella Manhattan

In 1985, after twenty-one years of intense socio-cultural repression, the military regime established in Brazil in 1964 came to an end, making it possible for fictional narrative to deal with themes prohibited by censorship, such as the issue of sexuality and homosexuality, due to the end of the strict supervision and prohibitions that were directed at the press and literature in general.

The fictional narrative has the characteristic of allowing the problematization of the reality experienced by subjects who until then were considered socially invisible, and allows issues relating to social minorities, such as homosexuality and female prostitutes, to be raised, favoring discussion and awareness of social problems.

As well as enabling the liberation of consciences, one of the social roles of literature is to denounce situations and events, shedding light on issues that have been little problematized, enabling the deconstruction of traditionalist and totalitarian values that segregate individuals, groups and peoples, reducing them to social marginality. Literature makes it possible to restructure various social discourses, including those dealing with the issue of sexuality and homosexuality. According to Foucault (2009), sexuality is constructed through experiences and has historical and socio-cultural origins.

Cinema, theater and music have all tackled the issue of the construction of gender identity and sexuality, allowing homosexuality to be portrayed and analyzed through a less discriminatory and exclusionary lens, as is the case in Stella Manhattan.

The narrative of *Stella Manhattan* takes place in October 1969, when, due to the creation of AI-5, Brazil was facing the harshest phase of the military regime. However, the story does not take place in Brazil, but on the island of Manhattan (NY), specifically on the urban periphery, where a Brazilian community of exiles lives. The protagonist of the novel, Eduardo da Costa e Silva, is a young Brazilian homosexual with a degree in Literature who is sent to New York after revealing his sexual orientation to his family.

In Manhattan, through the help of a friend of his father's, Colonel Valdevinos Vianna, Eduardo gets a job at the Brazilian consulate. Then, the introverted character begins a process of transformation, creates relationships of love and friendship and tries to lead a life in which he can more freely express his freedom, but he soon realizes that he can only be truly free, internally. After helping Colonel Valdevinos Vianna by renting an apartment in his own name in a poor neighborhood, which the military man, also a homosexual, uses as a meeting place for his sadomasochistic adventures, Eduardo faces serious problems: on the one hand, a clandestine group of Brazilian revolutionaries, and on the other, representatives of the Brazilian extreme right, who are also followed by the FBI, who suspect Eduardo of being a communist. Later, a man who looks like Eduardo is arrested, drunk and commits suicide in his cell after being raped by other prisoners. The book ends without Eduardo's whereabouts being explicitly and officially revealed.

The homosexual approach begins with the protagonist Eduardo, who during the day works at the Brazilian consulate and at night, on the fringes and outskirts of town, cross-dresses as Stella Manhattan, an effeminate and sensual transvestite.

When doing household chores, Eduardo assumes another identity, Bastiana, inspired by his childhood maid, called Sebastiana. The different attitudes he assumes give the impression that they are different people: "For not taking her to Woodstok that summer, Stella had forbidden Eduardo to go to the movies for a month and to have ice cream too [...]" (SANTIAGO,

1985, p. 21).

Homosexuality is also represented in the figure of Colonel Vianna, who during the day, at the consulate, or at home with his wife, is the influential and feared military man, prestigious for his services during political repression, and during the night, in the suburbs, he takes on the persona of the sadomasochistic Black Widow, who goes out every night, dressed in black clothes and leather boots, to give vent to her repressed desires and fantasies.

The homosexual approach in the military gives the impression that the colonel and the Black Widow are different people, and this duplicity of sexual identity in the same person was revealed mainly by the use of clothes that could characterize, externally of course, either the heterosexual image during the day, or the homosexual profile that the characters assumed at night:

> Vianna went on to enumerate the thousand difficulties he had in getting laid by a legal woman in New York, all the more so because he now liked heavy-set people and couldn't turn down blacks and Puerto Ricans either, and in New York if you're not dressed in character, there's nothing to it. [...] That's why he had some leather clothes hidden at home and no longer knew how to hide them without arousing his wife's suspicions (SANTIAGO, 1985, p. 55-56).

The figure of Colonel Vianna allows us to see that, in assuming two distinct behaviors related to sexuality, during the day the military man and at night the Black Widow, there is also the symbolic representation of the identities he assumed: as a colonel who represents the central power of the military regime, therefore, an active position of social control, and as the sadomasochistic Black Widow, possessing a passive behavior in relation to the sexual partners she chose.

The practice of sadomasochism reinforces the symbolism represented by the passivity of the figure of the Black Widow, because in addition to practicing homosexual relations, her preference for sadism counters the authority she represents when she personifies Colonel Vianna.

The language used in the work explores sexual desire, because homosexuals are denied the right to live out their dreams and fantasies completely, openly and explicitly in society, so there is only one way for them to express their homoaffective condition: sexual desire.

Homosexuality can also be seen in other characters in the book, such as Professor Anibal, a conservative who becomes a voyeur at night, watching his beautiful wife from the window of his apartment during sexual games with unknown men in the street; Marcelo, a revolutionary who seeks out male companions for his sexual games at night.

The freedom that Santiago's characters find at night allows us to reflect on the relationship between homosexuality and the space and time in which it is allowed to manifest itself, since it is possible to establish a strong link between the free manifestation of sexuality and the physical and temporal space in which these characters circulate.

Santiago's work presents this relationship between places, times and permitted behaviors, in which the night is the moment of liberation, of giving vent to the fantasies and dreams repressed during the day. Daytime can be seen as the moment when the clarity of prejudice and discrimination favors the surveillance and control of their lives by conservative society, which expresses its rejection in attitudes of violence and segregation.

The process of fragmentation of the characters divides their social identities and makes them inspectors of their own behavior, preventing their desires from being revealed, and this division, which takes them internally, can also be seen in the city, which is divided into places where homosexuals can freely give vent to their desires, and other environments where homosexuality is socially discriminated against. The city center is the place that imposes an attitude consistent with what is traditionally considered correct, and the periphery is the place where dreams, fantasies and inner impulses can be experienced, far from the disturbing and repressive surveillance of society.

Vigilance is responsible for the isolation of the characters and their search for belonging in peripheral spaces of refuge (the streets, squats and bars of the Village). Only in these places are marginalized desires allowed to be exposed. These places allow us to reflect on the homoeroticization of space, which can be seen in the growing number of social movements and LGBT spaces, so common today.

Silviano Santiago's experience abroad, especially during his PhD in Paris in 1968, may have contributed to the creation of his characters, due to the wealth of socio-cultural elements, and Santiago himself states that he drew on the Plastic Arts to compose the characters in Stella Manhattan .[4]

FINAL CONSIDERATIONS

As well as featuring characters linked to the theme of sexuality and having been published in 1985, a period that marks the end of the military dictatorship in Brazil, the two works cited in this article can be seen as an invitation from the authors for the reader to join them in a fight for the emancipation of women and for the recognition of the right to freely express sexuality, thus constituting two examples of engaged literature (SARTRE, 1993), in other words, based on a cause of social participation:

> A writer is engaged when he tries to become more lucidly and fully aware of having embarked, that is, when he makes the engagement pass, for himself and for others, from immediate spontaneity to the reflected plane. The writer is a mediator par excellence, and his engagement is mediation. But while it is true that one must account for his work from his condition, one must also remember that his condition is not only that of a man in general, but also, precisely, that of a writer (SARTRE, 1993, p. 61-62).

For Sartre, the process of uncovering the real world is what characterizes engagement, because it is through this discovery that the reader of a work is able to achieve their critical awakening, and this awakening, through literature, is a movement towards social change. According to him, the writer reveals

The world and, in particular, man for other men, so that they take full responsibility for the object thus laid bare. [...] In the same way, the function of the

[4]Information taken from an interview with Silviano Santiago on the Rede Globo website. Available at http://redeglobo.globo.com/globouniversidade/noticia/2013/07/em-entrevista-silviano-santiago-fala-sobre-sua-carreira.html.Acesso on January

30, 2017.

writer with whom no one can ignore the world and consider themselves innocent of it (SARTRE, 1993, p. 21).

Starting from the need to propose a reflection on the relationship between the manifestation of sexuality and social marginality, this book sought to analyze the two works taking into account the peripheral situation in which many people find themselves because of their sexual orientations and behaviors.

In this sense, despite the fact that Trevisan's protagonist frequents places such as motels, bars and cheap eateries, being socioculturally marginalized, her sexuality could be lived openly, there was no need to hide behind a social mask that would prevent her from being identified by other people.

On the other hand, although the characters in Stella Manhattan also frequent socially marginalized places, they only assume their homosexual status in specific places and at specific times, such as the Village's nightclubs, changing their behavior and posture according to the occasion: during the day they construct a heterosexual identity, more suited to the standards of behavior considered normal, and at night they deconstruct the identity assumed during the day and camouflage themselves by wearing clothes that better define their sexual orientation.

This constructive nature of the identity formation process is defended by Hall (2000) and Woodward (2000):

> The various social identities of class, gender, sexuality, ethnicity, race and others are socially constructed and performed simultaneously by people involved in the most diverse social practices (HALL, 2000; WOODWARD, 2000).

In a way, it can be said that Dalton Trevisan's prostitute protagonist is a realist - not in the sense of reproducing reality in an unbiased and objective way - an aesthetic utopia - but in the sense of representing ideas, prejudices and stereotypes that were impregnated in the Brazilian social imaginary and daily life at the time the novel was produced.

Trevisan shows Polaquinha's helpless and natural eroticism, but not just through an erotic discourse, but together with a discourse of power, which is realized through the erotic element. His book doesn't take a commercial view of sex, but rather shows that the path of prostitution chosen by the young woman was determined by the inequality of social forces, in which the patriarchal and sexist values that govern society relegate women to a socioculturally peripheral position.

This inequality of power and rights between men and women is confirmed by the philosopher Simone de Beauvoir when she says that "the world has always belonged to males" (BEAUVOIR, 2009, p.99). This hierarchy between the sexes is explained by the philosopher:

> [...] we see that when two human categories are present, each wants to impose its sovereignty on the other; when both are in a position to maintain their claim, a relationship of reciprocity is created between them, whether in hostility or friendship, always in tension. If one of them is privileged, it dominates the other and does everything it can to keep it oppressed. It is understandable, then, that the man should have wanted to dominate the woman (BEAUVOIR, 2009, p.99).

The parallel between the protagonists of the two works also allows us to see that in the career of the prostitute from Curitiba, her clothes only served as an accessory, a decoration for sexual programs, which differs from the purpose of Eduardo's and Colonel Vianna's clothing: they needed camouflage, because even the nightlife of the Village required its regulars to wear clothes that made it difficult to identify them.

These two works make it possible to reflect on sexual representations in the post-dictatorship period, considering that the literary text allows us to deconstruct the structures that try to control individuals' sexual behavior.

On the other hand, for Joao Silverio Trevisan, there is currently a certain "crisis of masculinity", caused partly by the achievements of the feminist movement, and partly by a socio-economic crisis of power:

> If, as Michel Foucault's followers would have it, forms of power historically determine gender differences, masculinity must be understood not only as a sexual determination of culture, but - based on this gender determination - as a way in which men have found to socially exercise their hegemonic power. In this sense, the current crisis of masculinity would be the crisis of male power (TREVISAN, 1998, p. 24).

Treating women as objects has always been part of patriarchy's strategy of domination. The "trafficking of women" that takes place, for example, in marriage is a male exchange whose primary objective is to strengthen an alliance between men: *"In the universe of the dominant male, the woman would be the bargaining chip within a relationship in which the real partner is another man"* (TREVISAN, 1998, p. 29).

The very control of sexuality creates a dispute between the sexes, delimiting what belongs to men and leaving women with what patriarchal society thinks belongs to them. In this sense, the social position of homosexuals is increasingly peripheral, they are increasingly silenced because they don't fit into the traditional male/female polarization.

BIBLIOGRAPHICAL REFERENCES

ALTHUSSER, L. *Ideologia e aparelhos ideologicos do Estado.* Lisbon: Presenga, 1980.

ANTONIO, J. *Abragado ao meu rancor: contos.* Guanabara Publishing House, 1986.

. *Malagueta, turkeys and bacanago.* Cosac & Naify, 2004.

BAKHTIN, M. *Popular culture in the Middle Ages and the Renaissance: the context of Francois Rabelais.* Trad. Yara Frateschi Vieira. Sao Paulo: Hucitec; Brasilia: Editora Universidade de Brasilia, 2008.

. *Aesthetics of verbal creation.* Translated by Paulo Bezerra. 4ª edition. Sao Paulo: Martins Fontes, 2003.

. *Marxism and the Philosophy of Language: Fundamental Problems of the Sociological Method in the Science of Language.* Translated by Michel Lahud, Yara Frateschi Vieira. 3rd edition. Sao Paulo: Hucitec, 1986.

. *Freudism: a critical sketch.* Translated by Paulo Bezerra. Sao Paulo: Perspectiva, 2007.

. *Problems of Dostoevsky's Poetry.* Translated by Paulo Bezerra. 4th edition. Rio de Janeiro: Forense Universitaria, 2008.

. *Questions of literature and aesthetics:* the theory of the novel. Translated by Aurora Fornoni Bernardini et al. 5th edition. Sao Paulo: Annablume, Hucitec, 2002.

BARTHES, R.; ARNICHAND, A.; LORENCINI, A. *O grau zero da escritura*, 1984.

BAUDELAIRE, C. *The Invention of Modernity (on art, literature and music). Translated by Pedro Tamen. Viseu: Relogio D'Agua Editores,* 2006.

BEAUVOIR, S. D. *O segundo sexo.* 2ª edition. Sao Paulo: Difusao Europeia do Livro, 2009.

DERRIDA, J. *Writing and difference.* University of Chicago Press, 1978.

DESCARTES, R. *Discourse on the method: And, meditations on first philosophy.* Yale University Press, 1996.

BENJAMIN, W. *Parigi capitale del XIXsecolo.* Torino, Einaudi, 1986.

ENGELS, F. *The origin of the family, private property and the state: work related to the investigations of L.H. Morgan.* Translated by Leandro Konder. 6ª edition. Rio de Janeiro: Civilizagao Brasileira, 1980 [1934].

FONSECA, R. *Happy New Year.* Nova Fronteira, 1975.

. *O cobrador e outros contos. Rio de Janeiro: Nova Fronteira,* 1979.

FOUCAULT, M. *History of sexuality I: the will to know.* Translated by Maria T. da C. Albuquerque and J.A.G. Albuquerque. 14th edition. Rio de Janeiro: Edigoes Graal, 1988.

. *Microphysics of power.* Org. and transl. Roberto Machado. 23rd edition. Rio de Janeiro: Edigoes Graal, 2007.

FREUD, S. *Jokes and their relationship to the unconscious. Complete Psychological Works of Sigmund Freud 8,* 1905[1969].

. *The unconscious. Complete works.* volume 14, 1915.

GOFFMAN, E. *Stigma: notes on the manipulation of damaged identity,* 1988.

GUTTING, G. *Foucault: a very short introduction.* Oxford: Oxford University Press, 2005.

GRIGOLETTO, E. Reflexoes sobre o funcionamento do discurso outro: de Bakhtin a analise do discurso. In ZANDWAIS, Ana (org.) *Mikhail Bakhtin: contributions to the philosophy of language and discursive studies.* Porto Alegre: Editora Sagra Luzzatto, 2005, p. 116-131.

HALL, S. *Cultural identity in postmodernity.* Translated by Tomaz Tadeu da Silva, Guacira Lopes Louro. 3. ed. Rio de Janeiro: DP&A, 1999.

. Who needs identity? In: SILVA, T. T. D.; HALL, S. (Org.) *Identidade e diferenga: a perspectiva dos estudos culturais.* 12 ed. Petropolis, RJ: Vozes, 2000, p. 103-133.

. *From the diaspora: identities and cultural media.* Translated by Adelaine La Guardia Resende et al. Belo Horizonte: Editora UFMG; Brasilia: UNESCO Representation in Brazil, 2003.

KAFKA, F. *The Trial.* Translation and afterword by Modesto Carone. *Sao Paulo: Companhia das Letras,* 1997.

LACAN, J. *The stage of the mirror as a shaper of the fungus of the "I".* In Writings. Jorge Zahar, Rio de Janeiro, 1998[1949].

. *The instantiation of the letter in the unconscious or reason since Freud.* In: Writings. Jorge Zahar, Rio de Janeiro, 1998[1957].

LACLAU, E. Poder y representation. *Politics, theory and contemporary culture,* 1993.

. *Democracy and the problem of power,* 2001.

LAURETIS, T. The technology of gender. In: HOLLANDA, B.H. *Tendencias e impasses: o feminismo como critica da cultura.* Rio de Janeiro: Rocco, 1994.

LOCKE, J. *Essay on human understanding.* 1999.

MEAD, G. H.; Morris, C. W. *Geist, Identitat und Gesellschaft*, 1970.

PARSONS, T. *Social system.* Routledge, 2013.

SANCHES NETO, M. *O artifico obsceno: visita a polaquinha.* Centro de Publicagoes, 1994.

SANTIAGO, S. *Vale quanto pesa: ensaios sobre questões politico-culturais.* Rio de Janeiro: Paz e Terra, 1982.

. *Stella Manhattan.* Rio de Janeiro, Nova Fronteira, 1985.

SARTRE, J. P. *What is literature?* Sao Paulo: Atica, 1993.

SPIVAK, G. C. *Can the subaltern speak?* 1ª edition. Translated by Sandra Regina Goulart Almeida; Marcos Pereira Feitosa; Andre Pereira. Belo Horizonte: Ed. UFMG, 2010.

TREVISAN, D. *A polaquinha.* Editora Record, 1985.

TREVISAN, J. S. *Seis bala num buraco so: a crise do masculino.* Rio de Janeiro: Record, 1998.

WILLIAMS, R. *Culture and society, 1780-1950.* Columbia University Press, 1983.

WOODWARD, K. Identity and difference: a theoretical and conceptual introduction. In: SILVA, T. T. D.; HALL, S. (Org.) *Identity and difference: a* *cultural studies perspective.*Petropolis, RJ: Vozes, 2000, p. 7-72.

MIX
Papier aus verantwortungsvollen Quellen
Paper from responsible sources
FSC® C105338

Printed by Books on Demand GmbH, Norderstedt / Germany